ZAP!

Future World

This edition first published in MMXVIII by
Book House

Distributed by Black Rabbit Books
P.O. Box 3263
Mankato, Minnesota 56002

Cataloging-in-Publication Data is available
from the Library of Congress

Printed in the United States
At Corporate Graphics,
North Mankato, Minnesota

9 8 7 6 5 4 3 2 1

ISBN: 978-1-911242-71-0

ZAP!

Future World

Richard & Louise Spilsbury

Contents

Look to the Future

What does the future hold? Will tourists be able to take weekend trips to the moon? Will people be able to climb aboard a submarine and take a tour of the deepest, darkest depths of an ocean? Will there be robots on the streets? The world is already full of things that, even 20 years ago, people would not have believed possible.

Virtual Reality

Virtual reality is an imaginary, **three-dimensional** world created by a computer that people can see when they wear special goggles. They can also wear special gloves and carry items so that when they enter and move about in the virtual world, they can interact with objects inside it.

Flying Skateboards

A prototype **levitating** hoverboard designed to work on a specially constructed skatepark was unveiled in 2015. It contains powerful magnets that allow it to float above a track hidden in the surface of the skatepark.

In virtual reality games, people are presented with a version of reality that is not really there but that creates an impression of reality.

This flying skateboard is nicknamed a "Slide."

In this book, we take a look at some of the things we could be using, seeing, or doing in the future and the people and machines that could make them happen.

The hoverboard uses the same technology as maglev trains.

Deep-Sea Diving

As people travel deeper and deeper below the surface of the ocean, it becomes colder, darker, and more mysterious. In this pitch-black world, there are creatures that few have ever seen and mountains and valleys higher and deeper than those found on land.

Thick wetsuits to keep out the cold and oxygen tanks to supply air allow divers to swim down only so far. To go really deep, divers need the right equipment. One day, ordinary people may be able to use **submersibles** to travel deep beneath the sea.

Submersibles

A submersible is a diving machine that people sit inside. As they go deeper, the mass of water above puts a lot of pressure on the human body. A submersible protects them from the **pressure** experienced deep underwater.

Thick, steel walls help to cope with high pressure deep underwater.

Propellers move the submersible.

Grab arms can pick up samples found in the deep.

Lights and cameras allow people to view and film what is around them.

The Mariana Trench is a valley on the ocean floor that is 6 miles (10 km) deep.

Animal Lights

Some deep-sea animals make their own light to find their way, attract **prey**, or communicate with other animals. Within their bodies, they combine chemicals that release light when they react together. This is similar to the way glow sticks work.

Avoiding the Bends

As divers go deeper, more air, which contains nitrogen, dissolves in their blood. If a diver ascends (goes up) too quickly, the nitrogen forms bubbles in the blood that can settle at joints, such as the knee. This causes immense pain and is known as "the bends." To avoid the bends, divers have to ascend slowly so that the nitrogen has time to escape into the lungs and to be breathed out safely.

Mariana Trench

The deepest **trench** in the world is the Mariana Trench near Japan. In 2012, a submersible dived there. It had more than 1,000 pounds (450 kg) of steel plates attached to it to help it sink. Once the submersible was deep enough, the plates dropped off so that the submersible would float back to the surface.

Only two submersibles have ever made it to the bottom of the Mariana Trench.

The Miracle of Flight

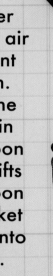

People have always looked up at the sky and dreamed about flying. At first, they copied birds and tried to make wings from wood or feathers. However, these did not work. To fly, people have to beat **gravity**—the **force** that pulls things to the ground and gives everything on Earth weight.

Lift is an upward pushing force that comes from the air. Wings provide flying machines with lift. Air blowing over the top of a curved wing pushes down less on the wing than the air that passes below the flat underside of the wing, so the wing is pushed upward.

A burner heats the air in a giant balloon. When the hot air in the balloon rises, it lifts the balloon and basket high up into the air.

Gliders

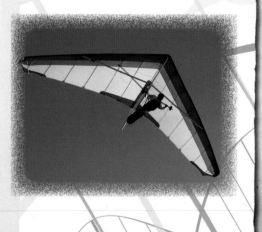

Gliders and hang gliders stay up in the air longer by finding a **thermal**. A thermal is an area of warm air that rises when heat comes off the land or buildings on Earth's surface. When in the air, **air resistance** slows them down.

Hot-Air Balloons

Things can also float when they are lighter than air. Hot air is lighter than cold air, so people use this principle to fly in hot-air balloons.

The record for the highest ever hot-air balloon flight is 69,852 feet (21,290 meters) high.

Jet Engines

The force that moves things forward is called **thrust**. Jet planes create thrust force by burning fuel in jet engines. Burning fuel makes hot gases. As these hot gases are released from the back of the engine and move backward, they create thrust that moves the plane forward.

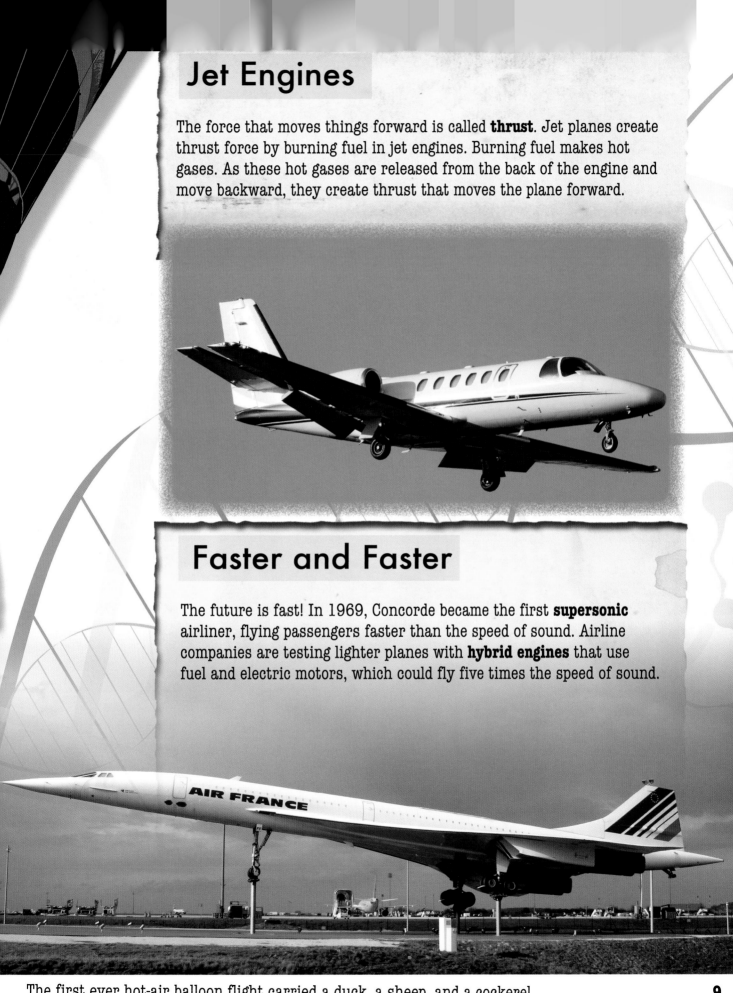

Faster and Faster

The future is fast! In 1969, Concorde became the first **supersonic** airliner, flying passengers faster than the speed of sound. Airline companies are testing lighter planes with **hybrid engines** that use fuel and electric motors, which could fly five times the speed of sound.

The first ever hot-air balloon flight carried a duck, a sheep, and a cockerel.

Space Odyssey

In the future, ordinary people might have the opportunity to visit space. Traveling in space is far more challenging than flying through the air. Rockets carrying a lot of equipment, cargo, and fuel are very heavy, so they need a lot of power to thrust them off Earth's surface into space.

Rockets burn fuel to force hot gases from their tail end at high speed. This provides them with the thrust they need to reach beyond Earth's gravity. To travel fast, rockets burn thousands of gallons of fuel each second.

Bye-Bye Boosters

Many rockets have a main engine and additional rocket boosters to help them reach space. The boosters are attached to the outside of the rocket. When these boosters have used up their fuel, they drop off and fall to Earth, where they land in oceans.

The fuel needed to launch a rocket usually weighs about 20 times more than the rocket itself.

In Orbit

When rockets escape Earth's **atmosphere**, there is no air, so there is no air resistance to slow them down. As a result, they keep moving. When a rocket's movement forward is equal to the pull of gravity, it keeps moving at the same distance around Earth without using power. This is called being in **orbit**.

Rockets are long and thin to reduce air resistance as they move through Earth's atmosphere.

Tail fins on the end of a shuttle help to keep it steady in the air.

Rockets carry oxygen because fuel needs air to burn and there is no air in space.

Space Tourism

Wealthy entrepreneurs are currently developing spacecraft that will allow members of the public to experience space travel. Passengers will be flown to the edge of Earth's atmosphere so that they can view our home planet as if they're astronauts orbiting in a satellite.

The first space shuttle was launched in 1981.

Surviving in Space

There is a chance that one day, people may be able to live in space. There are already people living for months on end on the International Space Station (ISS). Astronauts live there to carry out experiments inside and outside the station.

To build the ISS, the space shuttle carried large parts into space. The space shuttle also transported many of the things that astronauts need to survive, such as air, food, and water. On the ISS, there are small spacecraft that astronauts can use to escape back to Earth in case of an emergency.

The ISS orbits Earth 16 times a day.

The ISS has 16 huge **solar panels** to provide its electricity.

The ISS is the biggest object ever to fly in space.

The Vomit Comet

Before a mission, astronauts learn how to cope with **weightlessness** in space. The plane that they train in is known as a "vomit comet" because about one in three people are airsick when they first go in it.

Spacewalks

When astronauts go on a **spacewalk** they wear spacesuits to survive. When astronauts are in outer space, the spacesuit's strong, outer layer stops them from being injured by bits of space dust that move faster than bullets.

Helmets often have gold-lined **visors** to reflect sunlight away from an astronaut's eyes.

The backpack contains oxygen for astronauts to breathe.

Spacesuits have layers of **insulation** to stop astronauts from being too hot or too cold.

Space Gyms

On Earth, people's muscles and bones work against gravity all day to support their body weight. In space, the effects of gravity are so tiny that astronauts' bones and muscles often become weaker. This is why astronauts must exercise for at least 2 hours a day using machines with weights.

A group of 16 countries worked together to build the ISS.

What Do Astronomers Do?

Astronauts have flown into space, but most stars and **galaxies** are too far away to reach. People know about them only because of astronomers. Astronomers are scientists who use telescopes and other devices to study distant stars, moons, planets, and galaxies.

Astronomers use different types of telescopes. The Hubble Space Telescope is a huge telescope in space that takes pictures of planets, stars, and galaxies trillions of miles away.

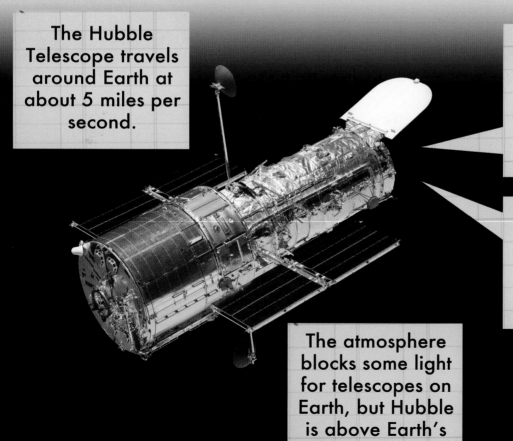

The Hubble Telescope travels around Earth at about 5 miles per second.

Hubble has mirrors that can collect about 40,000 times more light than the human eye.

Hubble has cameras that can see three different kinds of light.

The atmosphere blocks some light for telescopes on Earth, but Hubble is above Earth's atmosphere.

The Hubble Telescope is as long as a large school bus and weighs as much as two elephants.

How Telescopes Work

A refracting telescope works by bending light through a **lens** so that it forms an image. In a reflecting telescope, such as Hubble, it is the reflection from a curved mirror magnified by a secondary mirror that forms the image.

Space Wobbles

In 1995, the first planet ever seen outside our **solar system** was discovered. Astronomers identified it when they spotted a "wobble" in nearby stars. The wobble is the result of the stars being pulled by the gravity of a large object nearby.

Searching for Aliens

An Earth-sized planet, orbiting a star at a distance where liquid water could possibly exist, has been discovered. The discovery of Kepler-186f makes astronomers think that there could be planets out there similar to Earth. There could be alien life on these planets.

Space Facts

- There are 100,000,000,000 (100 billion) galaxies in Earth's universe.
- Earth's solar system is in a spiral galaxy called the Milky Way.
- Earth's sun is one of about 100 billion stars in the Milky Way.
- There are thousands of planets orbiting stars.

The Hubble Telescope is named after the famous astronomer Edwin P. Hubble.

Living on Another Planet

M ars is the only other planet in Earth's solar system where humans might be able to live. However, they cannot fly there yet. This is because they cannot launch a rocket big enough to take enough fuel for the six-month journey there and all the necessary supplies to survive on the planet. Life on Mars may be possible in the future, though.

Mars has a solid, rocky surface much like Earth's. It is very cold, and there is an ice cap at its south pole. Mars also has seasons and days as long as those on our planet.

Mars is 34.8 million miles (56 million km) away from Earth.

Mars is often called the red planet because its surface is covered in red rocks and sand.

It would take six months to reach Mars.

Mars rocks are red because the planet contains a lot of iron oxide (rust).

Space agencies believe they will be able to send a mission to land people on Mars by the 2030s.

Mars Rovers

Mars rovers are car-sized robots that are controlled by computers on Earth. They are used to explore the surface of Mars and collect samples of rock. Rovers use small amounts of power. This is because Mars has a thin atmosphere so there is little air resistance to push against.

Survival on Mars

Scientists are working on ways to help people survive on Mars. People will need to collect and melt ice on Mars to make liquid water to drink. They will need to make oxygen to breathe and grow plants for food. They will also have to construct buildings that protect them from the cold.

Biosphere 2

Biosphere 2 was a huge, sealed greenhouse for people, animals, and plants. It was built in the Arizona desert as an experiment in Mars survival. It was not a success. There were problems with amounts of food and oxygen, and many animal and plant species died.

Biosphere 2 had different **biome** areas, including a rain forest, an ocean, wetlands, grassland, and a desert.

Earth's next-nearest planet, Venus, is burning hot and has a poisonous atmosphere.

17

Star Trekking

The closest star system to Earth is called Alpha Centauri. It is more than 266,000 times farther away from us than our sun. It is impossible for humans to travel that far in today's space rockets because it would take tens of thousands of years to get there.

Voyager 1 is the most distant human-made object in space. This unmanned **space probe** flew past Jupiter, Saturn, and Saturn's large moon, Titan, before heading into **interstellar** space.

Voyager 1 carries greetings and a gold record of sounds and music, just in case an intelligent life-form finds it.

A signal from the ground, traveling at **light speed**, takes 17 hours to reach *Voyager 1*.

National Aeronautics and Space Administration (NASA) launched *Voyager 1* in September 1977.

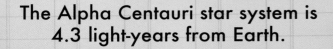

The Alpha Centauri star system is 4.3 light-years from Earth.

Light Speed

Distances in space are so vast that they are measured in light-years. A light-year is the distance traveled by light moving in a **vacuum** in the course of one year at a speed of 186,282 miles per second (299,792 km/s).

Gravity Assist Jupiter

Voyager 1 used gravity assist to help it on its way. Gravity assist is when a spacecraft orbits a planet and then suddenly uses its engines to speed up to leave the orbit at a particular moment. The planet's gravity gives the spacecraft more energy and flings it farther into space, like a slingshot.

Sleeper Ships

Perhaps in the future, scientists could send people on long missions by freezing them first. They could also send families, so later generations would eventually reach the destination. Other ideas include building gas stations in space where rockets could refuel.

Voyager 1 will run out of power and stop operating in 2025.

Remarkable
Robots

The robots shown in movies are usually humanoid robots—robots that look like humans. In fact, a robot is any moving machine that can automatically carry out a complex series of actions. They are usually programmed by remote control or by a computer.

There will probably be humanoid robots in the future, but armies, hospitals, and many other groups of people are already using remarkable robots of different shapes and sizes.

Controlling Robots

Robots often have cameras so that their operators can see what the robot sees. The operator can use a computer to control the robot's arms, engines, and wheels. Some robots can be preprogrammed to do a task, such as underwater robots that are sent below the ocean to investigate shipwrecks.

Factory Bots

The first factory robot was used in 1961. It just moved and stacked hot metal discs. Today, factory robots do all kinds of work. They have tools attached to arms that spray-paint cars and attach car doors. They can also sort out the wiring on tiny electrical circuits for mobile phones.

Armed Robotic Vehicles, or ARVs, may replace manned battle tanks in risky missions in the future.

Robot Exoskeletons

Some robots help people who use wheelchairs to walk again. They wear robotic **exoskeletons** over their clothes and attached to their limbs. The exoskeleton powers hip and knee movements to help people with spinal injuries stand up and walk.

Drones

Drones are flying robots. Armies use them to fly over areas of land to look for enemy troops or for injured soldiers in search-and-rescue operations. Many ordinary people also own drones and use them to take pictures or videos from the sky.

New robot replacement limbs may be able to help people to feel things.

Super-Speedy Machines

People are always looking at ways to make trains, boats, aircraft, and other vehicles travel faster. To achieve this, designers have to use **aerodynamics**—the way air and water behave when objects push through them at speed.

When boats travel forward at sea, they have to push the water ahead of them out of the way. The force they push against is water **resistance**. When planes fly through the air, air resistance tries to slow them down, so engineers need to build machines that can travel faster.

On the Road

To go faster, the force from the engine driving a car has to be greater than the forces trying to slow down the car. These forces include **friction** (caused by the road and tires rubbing against each other), air resistance pushing against the car, and, if traveling uphill, gravity is pulling it downhill.

Air resistance acts on the front of the car.

The thrust force from the engine pushes the car along.

Gravity pulls down on the car.

Friction acts between the road and the car tires.

The Bugatti Veyron can go 250 miles per hour (402 km/h).

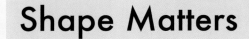

Shape Matters

Planes and racing cars are long and thin because there is less air resistance on thinner shapes than wider ones. This is because a smaller surface is pushing against the air. Cyclists also lean forward to make a more compact, **streamlined** shape to increase speed.

Wind Tunnels

Vehicle designers use **wind tunnels** to test the effect of air resistance on objects, such as cars. Inside a wind tunnel, air can be blown at different speeds past full-sized vehicles or scale models of airplanes and spacecraft. Dye or smoke can be added to the airstream in a wind tunnel so that the flow of air around the vehicle or cyclist can be photographed and studied.

The world's largest wind tunnel is in California. It is large enough to house a real airliner.

Perfecting the Parachute

When gravity pulls something down very quickly, the impact of hitting the ground can be dangerous. A parachute's slow descent allows the wearer to land safely. Italian artist and inventor Leonardo da Vinci drew a design for a parachute in his notebooks in 1483.

It wasn't long after an Australian pilot used a parachute to escape a damaged plane in 1916, during World War I, that they were being used by all air forces. Today, parachutes are also used for sport, to slow down airplanes on short runways, and to help spacecraft land on planets and moons.

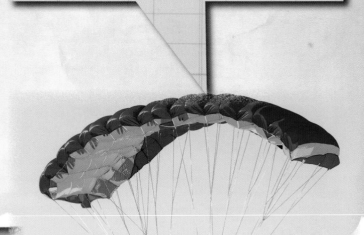

Parachutes have a wide, flat sheet of fabric that catches the air and pulls back on the object or person to which it is attached.

How to Use a Parachute

Most **skydivers** jump from between 4,000 feet (1,220 meters) and 12,000 feet (3,658 meters). When they first jump, they simply fall through the sky. Then, they open their parachutes to slow down their descent to about 1,000 feet (305 meters) per minute. This ensures a safe landing.

French aeronaut Jean Pierre Blanchard invented the first successful parachute in 1785.

Dandelion seeds have "parachutes" to help them drift to new places grow.

When a seed lands, the parachute breaks off, and the seed embeds in the soil ready to grow.

Nature's Parachutes

Baby spiders shoot out several thin strands of silk to catch the wind like a parachute. They use their silken parachutes to carry them to new places to find food. Dandelion seeds grow on a thin stalk topped with a circle of white wispy threads that catch the air and allow the seed to be carried away.

Parachuting from Space

In 2012, Felix Baumgartner claimed the world record for the highest skydive. He leapt from 127,953 feet (39,000 meters) and floated to the edge of Earth's atmosphere in a capsule beneath a giant **helium** balloon. It took him 9 minutes, 3 seconds to descend to Earth.

Felix Baumgartner opened his parachute when he was 8,255 feet (2,516 meters) above land.

Making an Electric Car

In the future, there could be millions of electric cars on the world's roads. An electric car uses electricity stored in a battery pack that powers an electric motor and turns the vehicle's wheels.

Burning gasoline and diesel fuels causes pollution and releases gases that are linked to **global warming**. Electric cars do not produce heat-trapping gases and pollution when driven. However, the power stations that create the electricity do, and extracting **fossil fuels**, such as coal, to make electricity does, too.

Types of Energy

An electric car uses a battery to convert chemical energy into kinetic (movement) energy in electric motors. Gasoline or diesel cars burn fuel to convert chemical energy into kinetic energy.

New Forms of Energy

An alternative future power source for cars is fuel cells. Fuel cell vehicles combine hydrogen and oxygen gases to produce electricity. This is then used to run the motor. Fossil fuels will run out one day, but hydrogen can be obtained from Earth's plentiful supplies of water.

An electric car's batteries can be recharged using electricity from a wall socket or a special charging unit.

In 1997, the Toyota Prius became the first car with a hybrid engine to sell in large numbers.

Hybrid Cars

- Hybrid cars use batteries to power an electric motor that drives the car in city traffic.
- They use gasoline engines to drive the car at high speeds on highways and to power the car if the battery runs out.
- The gasoline engine is used to recharge the motor's battery.
- When more power is needed, the gasoline engine and the electric motor can work together.

The Tesla Model S is a completely electric car. It can go from 0 to 60 miles per hour (96.5 km/h) in 5.4 seconds. It creates zero emissions.

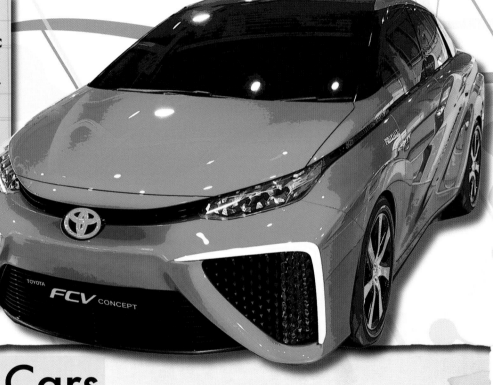

Electric Cars

Pros

- cheaper to run and maintain

- nonpolluting when driven

- quiet engine

Cons

- can go only around 75 miles (120 km) before needing to recharge

- recharging is time-consuming

Formula E is a new kind of car racing only for electric racing cars.

Musical Marvels

Today, people can listen to almost any music they like, whenever or wherever they want, thanks to new technologies and handheld devices. The popularity of websites, such as YouTube and SoundCloud, has made finding new music easier than ever before.

The Internet also makes promoting new music easy. New artists that would have had to sign record deals in the past can now share their music via social networks. They can distribute it using platforms such as iTunes. However, the ways in which most music is made have stayed the same.

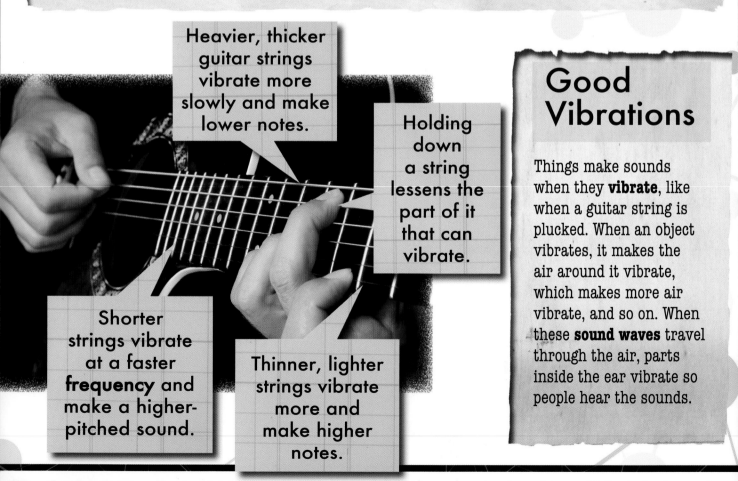

Heavier, thicker guitar strings vibrate more slowly and make lower notes.

Holding down a string lessens the part of it that can vibrate.

Shorter strings vibrate at a faster **frequency** and make a higher-pitched sound.

Thinner, lighter strings vibrate more and make higher notes.

Good Vibrations

Things make sounds when they **vibrate**, like when a guitar string is plucked. When an object vibrates, it makes the air around it vibrate, which makes more air vibrate, and so on. When these **sound waves** travel through the air, parts inside the ear vibrate so people hear the sounds.

Smoke alarms vibrate at high frequency, about 3,000 times a second, making a high-pitched sound.

High and Low Sounds

Whether a sound is high or low depends on how quickly something vibrates. When the string on a guitar vibrates very quickly it plays a high note. When the string on a guitar vibrates slowly, it plays a low note. The number of vibrations per second is called the frequency of the sound. Larger musical instruments vibrate more slowly. This is because vibrations take a long time to move through them, so they have a slower frequency and a lower pitch.

Wind instruments, such as a tuba, make sound when the air blown inside them vibrates.

Musical Laptops

As well as making music on instruments, people can make music on computers. There are apps and programs that allow people to compose songs by using prerecorded **loops** and adding **mixes**, instruments, and other sound effects. Anyone can be a DJ today.

Elephants make some very low-frequency sounds that are too low for humans to hear.

Glossary

Aerodynamics How well something moves through the air.

Air resistance The force of air that slows down a car or an airplane.

Atmosphere The band of gases surrounding Earth, which ends when space begins.

Biome A specific environment, such as desert, that is home to living things suited for that place and climate.

Exoskeletons Structures that support an animal's body from the outside.

Force A push or pull on an object.

Fossil fuels Coal, oil, gas, or other fuels that formed from the remains of living things that died millions of years ago.

Frequency The number of vibrations in a sound or the number of times that a sound wave vibrates in a second.

Friction The force that slows down movement when one surface moves over another.

Galaxies Systems of millions or billions of stars, gas, and dust, held together by gravity.

Global warming A gradual increase in the overall temperature of Earth's atmosphere linked to increased levels of pollution and gases like carbon dioxide in the air.

Gravity The force that pulls objects toward Earth or other very large, heavy objects.

Helium A gas that is lighter than air.

Hybrid engines Engines that combine a gasoline engine with another type of engine, like an electric motor.

Insulation Material that stops heat or cold passing through it.

Interstellar Situated between the stars.

Lens A clear curved piece of glass or plastic used to make things look clearer, smaller, or bigger.

Levitating Floating just above the ground.

Light speed The speed at which light travels.

Loops Repeating sections of sound.

Mixes Making a piece of music by combining a number of separate recordings.

Orbit The path one object in space takes around another.

Pressure Pushing force.

Prey An animal hunted and eaten by another animal.

Resistance A force that works against another force to slow it down or stop it.

Satellites Electronic devices placed in orbit around Earth or another planet.

Skydivers People who jump from an aircraft and fall for as long as possible before opening parachutes.

Solar panels Panels that use the energy in sunlight to make electricity.

Solar system The sun and the planets in orbit around it, including Earth.

Sound waves Vibrations in the air heard as sound.

Space probe An unmanned robotic spacecraft that explores space.

Spacewalk Walking or moving outside of a spacecraft while it is in space.

Streamlined Shaped to reduce air resistance and move through the air easily and quickly.

Submersibles A small diving machine that people sit inside.

Supersonic Faster than the speed of sound.

Thermal An upward current of warm air.

Three-dimensional Describes an object that has height, width, and depth, like any object in the real world.

Thrust A force usually produced by an engine to push a vehicle forward.

Trench A deep valley or hole in the ground.

Vacuum A place where there is nothing at all, not even air.

Vibrate To repeatedly move forward and backward or up and down very quickly.

Visors Parts on the front of helmets that can be pulled down to cover the face.

Weightlessness Having little or no weight.

Wind tunnels Spaces used to test the flow of air past objects such as aircraft.

Index